P9-DMT-278

A Life Worth Living
Course Manual

Cook Ministry Resources *a division of Cook Communications Ministries International*
Colorado Springs, Colorado/Paris, Ontario

For many, the *Alpha*™ course represents the first steps in the Christian life, and many new Christians will end the course asking, "What happens next?"

A Life Worth Living is aimed specifically at those who are starting out in the Christian life and is an excellent follow-up course to *Alpha*™ .

Cook Ministry Resources is a division of Cook Communications Ministries International (CCMI). In fulfilling its mission to encourage the acceptance of Jesus Christ as personal Savior and to contribute to the teaching and putting into practice of His two great commandments, CCMI creates and disseminates Christian communication materials and services to people throughout the world.

This edition issued by special arrangement with HTB Publications, Brompton Road, London, England SW7 1JA.

Unless otherwise indicated, biblical quotations are from THE HOLY BIBLE, NEW INTERNATIONAL VERSION Copyright © 1973, 1978, 1984 by the International Bible Society. Used by permission of Zondervan Publishing House. All rights reserved.

Text illustrations by Charlie Mackesy

ISBN 0-7814-5556-1

Contents

Chapter 1
NEW HEART
Philippians 1:1-11

Introduction

Five remarkable features of the letter:

    The place

    The people

    The purpose

    The pleasure

    The preamble

I. Confidence in the power of God

(vss. 3-6)

Joy and thanks

Church founded on signs and wonders—circa A.D. 52

1) Paul's vision

• Asia, Bithynia—doors seemed to be shut

2) An extraordinary conversion

• No synagogue in Philippi, but a prayer meeting by the river

• Lydia opened her heart to Jesus and opened her home to Paul

Notes

Notes

3) Evil cast out

- •Slave girl damaged by involvement with occult

"In the name of Jesus Christ I command you to come out of her!"

(Acts 16:18)

- •Fury of owners: Paul and Silas arrested and flogged

- •Paul and Silas praised God in prison

4) The power of God

- •Earthquake in prison

- •Jailer asks *"What must I do to be saved?"*

—an evangelistic opportunity!

What about us?

- •The promise of eternal life —starts now and goes on forever (John 10:28)

•God will bring to completion His work in our life

II. Compassion for the people of God (vss. 7-8)

Paul was not a "soft touch"

(e.g. Acts 16, and his dealings with the Roman authorities)

1) He had a deep love for the Philippians

• *"I have you in my heart..."* (vs. 7)

2) He felt very close to them

• "Affection" = *splagchna*— upper intestines, heart, lungs, liver, thought to be the source of deep emotion

• The nearest equivalent would be "compassion." Paul had a heart of compassion—the heart of Jesus

• *"His heart throbs with the heart of Christ..."*
J.B. Lightfoot

3) He felt responsible for their conversion

Notes

_____

_____

_____

_____

_____

_____

_____

_____

_____

_____

_____

_____

_____

_____

_____

_____

_____

_____

_____

_____

_____

_____

_____

_____

_____

_____

_____

Notes

III. Concern for the priorities of growth (vss. 9-11)

An 11-12 year gap between Paul's visit and his letter

The church had flourished and grown both numerically and in maturity

Three prayers for growth:

1) • Love—"Abound more and more..." (vs. 9)

   • The first and most important quality

2) • Understanding of God

   • Understanding of each other

3) • Holiness of life

   • "pure" = unmixed

   • Inner purity

   • Blameless = "without giving offense"

This kind of life will be fruitful, "the fruit of righteousness"

Conclusion

1) Three things that will last:

- Faith—confidence in God's power

- Love—compassion for the people of God

- Hope—concern for the principles of growth

2) Most common word is "*Christ*"

- His power

- His compassion

- His fruit

3) He brings "*glory and praise to God*" (vs. 11)

Recommended reading
A Life Worth Living
Nicky Gumbel
Cook Ministry Resources
1-800-36-ALPHA

Notes _stripped & on_ _incarcerated death row._ ## Chapter 2
NEW PURPOSE
Philippians 1:12-30

Paul an Ambassador in chains

His Passion to Preach Christ

How to - Create Possibilities ✓

In chains for Christ

chained to Guards 4 @ day

He Wrote letters - made

History (: Bible) =

children (wife of John Wesley

raised & schooled them

& farmed.

12-14

Introduction

"What has happened to me..."
(vss. 12-19)

Acts 21-28:

False accusation

Mob violence

In the torture chamber

In the dock

Assassination plot

In the hands of a tyrant

Shipwreck

Paul rejoices because his supreme calling in life is being fulfilled, i.e., to _"advance the gospel"_ (vs.12)— "Advancement in spite of obstructions and dangers which would block the traveller's path"

I. Gospel possibilities (vss. 12-14)

Soldiers from the palace guard constantly chained to Paul

1) He made the most of where God had put him

- Spoke

- Wrote letters

- Directly—guards all heard

- Indirectly—others encouraged

2) Inspired to speak about Jesus more freely

- "Most of the brothers and sisters..." (vs. 14)

3) What about us?

- Opportunities to serve Christ are here and now

II. Gospel priorities (vss. 15-18b)

LOVE

Sadly, even among Christians, envy, rivalry, and selfish ambition exist

Two responses to Paul's imprisonment:

1) "We must get on with the work now"—good will

2) "Now is our chance to outdo Paul"—envy and rivalry

Paul's view:

"What does it matter . . . Christ is preached"

Notes

eternally condemned.

a) The message (does matter) *or be*
(Galatians 1:8)

- Not all roads lead to God!

b) The means do matter

- The end does not always justify the means

c) The motives are less important

- We should try to get them right, but many come to Christ for the wrong motives

III. Gospel purpose for living

(vss. 19-26)

1) Paul's purpose for living was to know Christ and to make Him known to others

2) He was not remotely worried about death—as long as Jesus was honored

- Death is *"gain"* (vs. 21) and *"better by far..."* (vs. 23)

3) Equally, *"to live is Christ"*

to DIE IS GAIN.

4) Extension of his life meant ✳ *"fruitful labor"* (vs. 22)

5) Paul's life necessary for Philippians' progress *"progress and joy"* (vss. 25-26)

- The ultimate purpose of life in Jesus Christ. In Him true joy is to be found

IV. Gospel pattern of life

(vss. 27-30)

1) Not just words but actions

A lifestyle different from those around

- Citizens of heaven

- Relationships—standing together in the face of attack

2) All impossible without two things (vs. 19)

- Prayer

- Help of the Spirit

Conclusion

Unite in the task of advancing the Gospel:

- Create possibilities for the Gospel

- Concentrate on the Gospel priority

- Center our lives on the Gospel purpose

- Conduct our life according to the Gospel pattern

Notes

"Christians" don't "fight" on another or you leave yourselves vulnerable to the enemy.

Recommended reading

The Household of God
Lesslie Newbigin
Paternoster Press
0853649359
(Theological book for the advanced reader)

Chapter 3

NEW ATTITUDE
Philippians 2:1-11

Notes

Preaching Gospel is Preaching Christ

Be one in purpose ~~is~~ and love.

Sons & Daughters of GOD. AS Such. We envelope others IN that love

Introduction

1) Paul's situation ✓ *12*

• Chained, guarded, unjustly accused, deprived of comfort, facing early death, lost his freedom, lost his ministry

2) Paul's attitude

• 99% happy! The 1% had nothing to do with his own interests but the Philippians'

lack of unity destroys

3) Paul feared disunity. His joy would be *"complete"* if this fear were allayed *right on.*

• Euodia and Syntyche —no great split but Paul saw the danger signs *Beware*

• The appeal is made with passion and reason (vs. 1)

4) Four grounds for unity

• All Christians are united in ✓ Christ

• God's love: As we experience God's love, we will show it to others

- The (same) Holy Spirit lives in each of us
- Christian love *"...tenderness and compassion..."*

5) Three types of unity (vs. 2)

- Mind— *"...like-minded..."* (vs. 2) Not necessarily agreeing on everything, but same approach and attitude

- Emotions— *"...same love..."* (vs. 2) Not necessarily loving the same things, but same attitude of love

- Will— *"...one in spirit and purpose..."* (vs. 2) Same ultimate goal and purpose—God's glory— even if not always agreeing on how to get there

I. Wrong attitudes (vss. 3-4)

Def: rivalry —

1) Selfish ambition (vs. 3) √

- There is nothing wrong with the desire to succeed, as long as it is subordinated to the will and glory of God

- Ambition should be for Christ— noble ambition

2) Self-importance (vs. 3)

- The opposite of *"vain conceit"* is humility

Notes

Have you a need for approval, admiration as imp. name—

NEW ATTITUDE

Fore Vida Quote = Def. Christianity, Love is not self. imp.

"In humility consider others better than yourselves" (vs. 3)

•Not more gifted or morally better, but more important

3) Self-centeredness (vs. 4)

•The Christian life should change our focus—look to interests of others

•How do we treat our family, our neighbors, our friends, our colleagues, members of our church?

•Who is at the center of our conversations, thoughts, prayers? GOD & OTHERS.

II. Right attitudes (vss. 5-11)

Probably an early Christian hymn

The mind of Christ displays the opposite of selfish ambition, self-importance and self-centeredness

1) Let go His natural status (vs. 6)

•Exchanged the status of God for that of man

•Climbed down the ladder of achievement (not up!)

•Demoted Himself: became downwardly mobile

•Jesus was ambitious and determined, but not for Himself

this attitude ours by inheritance.

opposite of social climbing

2) Let go His social status (vs. 7)

• The King of kings and Lord of lords *"made himself nothing"*

• Not social climbing but social descending

• Demoted Himself to status of a slave

• Opposite of vain conceit and self importance

3) Let go His legal status (vs. 8)

• Humbled Himself still further by giving up His right to life

• Died on Roman cross— *"obedient to death"* (vs. 8): He died so that we might have life

• Exposed to mockery of crowd by dying as a slave. He became a slave so that we might be set free

• He became like us so that we might become like Him: He exchanged the position of highest on high for our deepest depth

The path of greatness in God's eyes (vss. 9-11)

Humility comes before exaltation (Mark 10:43-44; Luke 14:11; 1 Peter 5:5-6)

Conclusion

Follow Jesus' example—servant of God

Follow Paul's example—servant of Christ

Recommended reading
What's So Amazing About Grace?
Philip Yancey
Harper Collins
0310218624

Chapter 4
NEW RESPONSIBILITIES

Philippians 2:12-18

Introduction

Take responsibility seriously

He set us Free so.

TAKE ## I. Our responsibility for our lives

(vss. 12-13)

Salvation brings freedom from guilt, addiction, and fear—we can then experience and show love

Freedom and responsibility are inseparable

It is our responsibility to hear God's call, discover our gifts, and use them

"Fear and trembling"—importance of task and opportunity

Possibility of saved soul and wasted life. Need to surrender will to God and He will enable us to fulfill our potential

Notes

Set the Mark to achieve — THEN Go Forth in his love & the Power H-S & Gods Promises & To Do all forever for Christ in all areas that your Life Touches

Work out your Salvation as God works in you energizing you

To become Blameless or pure

Live a Life that appears (seems) to be Pure

Hold out to all the Good News That Christ died for our Salvation

II. Our responsibility to society (vss. 14-16a)

"Crooked"—warped activities

"Depraved"—distorted values

Christians called to be noticeably different:

1) Lifestyle

• *"Without complaining or arguing"*

"Praise—the fruit of lips that confess his name" (Hebrews 13:15)

• *"Blameless and pure"*

• Different from the world around *"shine like stars"*

• We live in a dissatisfied society that desperately needs God—we have good news

2) Lips

• *"hold out the word of life"*

III. Our responsibility to the church (vss. 16b-18)

1) Athletic metaphor: "run . . . labor"

2) Sacrificial metaphor: "poured out" for them

• Paul's reaction to hard work: he rejoices and asks them to rejoice also

Conclusion

Responsibility to work out what following Jesus means

- For our lives

- For society

- For other Christians

Recommended Reading

The Street Children of Brazil
Sarah de Carvalho
Hodder & Stoughton
0340641649

C.S. Lewis = Quote:?

Chapter 5
NEW FRIENDSHIPS
Philippians 2:19-30

Letter of friendship

Introduction

Friendship is at the heart of Christianity:

> Creation
> Fall
> Redemption
> New creation

Friendship is undervalued in our society *There is a hunger for friendship with God & Fellowman.*

I. Genuine interest

1) Paul and Timothy

- *"My son whom I love"* (1 Corinthians 4:17)

- Paul and Timothy suffered together

- Paul used Timothy to send information, advice, and encouragement (vss. 19-23)

- Timothy was loyal, reliable, and took a "genuine interest" (vs. 20)

2) Paul and Epaphroditus

- Loyal friend to Paul and
  Philippians

- Epaphroditus seriously ill, but
  only concerned because he did
  not want to burden others

3) Friendship requires genuine
love for others

- We make friends out of love—
  love leads to evangelism

II. Common focus

Interests of Jesus Christ (vs. 21)

All friendship arises out
of common interest,
but Christian friendship
is in a different league

- Brothers (vs. 25)

- Deep trust
  (1 Thessalonians 3:2)

- Encourage one
  another

- Pray for one another

III. Serving together

1) Friendship is the basis of a
flourishing church

- Serve together *"in the work
  of the gospel"* (vs. 22)

Notes

2) Jesus' closest friends were those He worked with

- Work together (vs. 25)

IV. Risks and battles

"Fellow-soldier" (vs. 25)

1) Christian life is not easy— friendship may mean taking risks

- Epaphroditus showed reckless courage on behalf of Paul

2) Jesus was

- Betrayed

- Deserted

- Disowned as an embarrassment

- Rejected

3) Jesus remained

- Totally committed (John 15:13)

- Totally open (John 15:11)

4) Sunday school lesson on joy in friendships

Jesus

Others

Yourself

Conclusion

True friendships made possible
through Jesus' work and example

(Philippians 2:6-11)

(John 15:13-15)

Recommended reading

The Four Loves
C.S.Lewis
Harcourt Brace & Company
0-1513-2916-8

Notes

_____

_____

_____

_____

_____

_____

_____

_____

_____

_____

_____

_____

_____

_____

_____

_____

_____

_____

_____

_____

_____

_____

_____

Notes

Chapter 6

NEW CONFIDENCE

Philippians 3:1-11

Introduction

types

Somewhat in certain circumsta

Worldly confidence is often based on pride, power, intelligence, money, success, etc.

On the other hand, many lack confidence, feel worthless, are inwardly afraid, and have a sense of inadequacy and insecurity

—Should we be confident?

—How can we be confident?

—What is true confidence?

—What is false confidence?

I. False confidence (vss. 1-6)

Warning—not to be deceived by false teaching on circumcision (vs. 2)

Our confidence and assurance (of salvation) are not found in outward signs, but in faith in Christ (vs. 3)

Scavenger Dogs people

Paul had many reasons to put confidence in worldly things

Seven reasons for false confidence

- Confidence from birth (vss. 4-5)

  1) Outward marks of religion—circumcised on the eighth day

  2) National privilege—*"...of the people of Israel..."*

  3) Family background—impeccable *"...tribe of Benjamin..."*

  4) Racial purity—*"...Hebrew of Hebrews..."*

- Confidence from personal achievements (vss. 5-8)

  5) Religious—*"...in regard to the law, a Pharisee..."*

  6) Sincerity—sincere in theory: energetic in practice *"...persecuting the church..."*

  7) Led a good life—*"as for legalistic righteousness, faultless..."*

Before conversion Paul had no bad conscience or inner conflict. Hard to see anything wrong in himself—compared well with those around him. Many feel the same today

But Paul rejects with disgust all the things he once thought were valuable

Notes

2 Cor. 5:21
Eph. 2:8, 10

Knowing Christ gives us true confidence before God. He went to the Cross for the sin of Man. Now approach God with Confidence. He will receive you with LOVE

"rubbish" (vs. 8)—literal translation —waste foods confined to rubbish heap, or human excrement rejected by body as not possessing nutritive qualities—all useless compared to something far greater. So much of what we value is "rubbish" also

II. True confidence (vss. 7-9)

1) New relationship (vss. 7-8)

Paul encountered Jesus and continued a vital, lively relationship

2) New righteousness (vss. 8-9) (Romans 3:20)

"Righteousness" = right relationship with God

- It is a gift *"from God"* (vs. 9)

- It is made possible through the cross (Romans 3:21-26)

- It gives us confidence for both the present and the future

- We receive it by faith (vs. 9)

Conclusion

We have confidence

- Before others
(2 Corinthians 5:6)

- Before God (Ephesians 3:12)

Our new confidence is from God
(vs. 9)

The person whose life is centered on
Christ will grow in confidence. The
best place to be is in the loving and
supportive community of the
Christian church

Recommended reading

Knowing God
J.I. Packer
InterVarsity Press
0-8308-1651-8

Notes

6 P.M. Lounge.

NEW AMBITIONS
Philippians 3:10-21

Introduction

1) Should a Christian be ambitious?

- Some Christians hotly pursue worldly ambitions, while others give up all desire to succeed

- Paul was fiercely ambitious both before and after his conversion, but for different things

2) There are essentially two controlling ambitions:

- Our own glory

- God's glory

I. Our glory: self-centered ambition
(vss. 17-21)

Paul's priority: Jesus and those who do not know Christ before himself (2 Corinthians 6:4-7)

The world's priority: themselves before Jesus—consciously or unconsciously

Paul understands that their "*...destiny is destruction...*" (vs. 19) Do we grasp that?

1) Their appetites dictate their lives— "*...their god is their stomach...*"

(vs. 19)—personal satisfaction and sensuality

The body itself is not evil—Jesus took human flesh

God gave us all things *"richly to enjoy,"* including taste, touch, sight, smell, hearing, sexuality

We must, however, keep these things within the limits God has set. They themselves are not gods, but gifts from God

2) They boast when they should blush

3) They take pleasure in the wrong things

Notes

"...where your treasure is, there your heart will be also..."

(Matthew 6:21)

TEST: What do we think about when our minds are neutral?

II. God's glory: Jesus-centered ambition (vss. 10-16)

1) Paul's ambition is to know Jesus Christ (vs. 10)

- He means more than intellectual knowledge: an exciting, exhilarating, intimate union

2) Knowing Christ entails knowing _"... the power of his resurrection..."_ (vs. 10)

- The Holy Spirit raised Jesus from the dead (Romans 8:11). The same Spirit lives in us and gives us:

—Power to live like Jesus

—Power to minister to others

3) Suffering (vs. 10)

- Not a penalty but a privilege

- Practical result of living the Christian life

- For some—severe persecution

- For all—taking up our cross daily

4) Our destiny (vs. 11) We are living between two resurrections—Christ's and ours (Philippians 1:20-23; 3:20-21)

5) But it has not happened yet—we are not yet perfect (vs. 12)

- Paul is single-minded and determined (vs. 13)

- He has one overriding ambition (but other areas of life are not neglected)

- He looked to the future—not dwelling on past successes or failures

We are to be like Paul and to *"press on toward the goal to win the prize"* (vss. 13-14)

Conclusion

Christians are citizens of heaven. Just as Jesus was transformed from a "lowly" human being when He was raised from the dead, so will we be. Our bodies will be transformed like His glorious body (vs. 21)

Everyone is on one of two paths

- Two destinations—heaven or destruction

Notes

- Two powers at work—power of Holy Spirit or grip of human appetites

- Two lifestyles—willing to share Christ's suffering or seeking own comfort and ease

- Two gods—our Lord Jesus Christ or our "stomach"

- Two attitudes to Jesus—friendship at intimate level or enemy of the Cross

- Two ambitions—His glory or our own

Recommended reading

Born Again
Charles Colson
Flemming H. Revell Co.
0-8007-9172-X

Chapter 8
NEW RESOURCES

Philippians 4:1-9

Introduction

* 1) Where will you be in ten years time?

2) How can we "stand firm" in the Lord? (vs. 1)

3) Paul's advice to the Philippians based on love for them

- Friend
- Brother
- Loved and longed for
- Joy and crown

"Stand firm" (as a soldier in battle or in the amphitheater)

Four secrets of standing firm in the Lord:

I. Watch your relationships with other Christians (vss. 2-3)

1) Personality clashes lead people away from God

Notes

_____

_____

_____

_____

_____

_____

_____

_____

_____

_____

_____

_____

_____

- Euodia and Syntyche

- Disagreements, disunity, and unforgiveness destroy faith

2) Christian friendships are vital for standing firm

sort out problems
forgive

II. Watch your relationship with the Lord (vss. 4-7)

1) Enjoy the Lord (vs. 4) even in times of trouble and persecution

2) Expect the Lord (vs. 5)

Gentleness/graciousness is the opposite of abrasiveness/contention

"The Lord is near" *He'll fight for you*

- In time—He is coming

- In space—speak to Him, listen to Him, love Him

3) Entreat the Lord (vss. 6-7)

With thanksgiving

Prayer and worry do not sit easily together. Take your anxiety to God (vss. 6-7)

The peace of God transcends all understanding

- We cannot understand it

- Others cannot understand it

Prayer
petition
with Thanksgiving

"Guard"—a military word: God's peace protects us from attacks and keeps us close to the Lord

III. Watch your unseen thoughts (vs. 8)

1) Importance of thoughts

- Different from the world around

- Thoughts—action—habit—character—destiny

- The way to get wrong thoughts out is to get right thoughts in

- A tree is only as strong as its roots

IV. Watch the example of other Christians (vs. 9)

1) Great men and women of God inspire us

(Hebrews 11)

"Received" is a technical term for receiving an authoritative tradition (1 Corinthians 11:23, 15:3)

But we must look primarily at Jesus (Hebrews 12:2)

Notes

(handwritten notes:) σύλληψις

Stood firm for 86 yrs in the Lord with Dignity & Grace

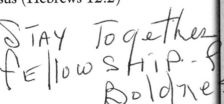

STAY Together in fellowship for Boldness & courage a dignity Grace

Notes

Put into practice what we have learned from others

"...The God of peace will be with you..."

Conclusion

1) We are cut off from God by unforgiveness, quarreling, worry, sinful thoughts, and following bad examples

2) We stay close to God through forgiveness, unity, prayer, thankfulness, right thoughts, and following good examples

Watch

- Our relationship with God
- Our relationship with others
- Our thought life
- Example of others

Then we will "stand firm in the Lord" into eternal life

Recommended reading
Paul's Letter to the Philippians
Gordon Fee
Eerdmanns
0802825117

(Theological book for the advanced reader)

Chapter 9
NEW GENEROSITY
Philippians 4:10-23

Introduction

Paul thanks the Christians at Philippi for sending him money via Epaphroditus

The threefold joy of giving:

I. Generous giving brings joy to others (vss. 10-16)

1) Paul has been made happy by their concern

- But in some ways he doesn't need the money

- *"...not...in need..."* (vs. 11)

2) Paul has learned the secret of contentment (this did not come naturally—before he was a Christian he used to "covet")

- Some think the secret of contentment is to have everything we want

"whatever the circumstances... to be in need..., to have plenty..., well fed..., hungry..."

Notes

_____
_____
_____
_____
_____
_____
_____
_____
_____
_____
_____
_____
_____
_____
_____
_____
_____
_____
_____
_____
_____
_____
_____
_____
_____
_____
_____

II. Generous giving brings joy to the lives of those who give
(vss. 17-18)

"Whoever sows sparingly will also reap sparingly, and whoever sows generously will also reap generously" (2 Corinthians 9:6)

Giving is a good investment in the Kingdom of God: it brings great profit to both the giver and the recipient

- Whatever we give God multiplies

- Whatever we give (time, gifts, money) we are blessed both in this life and into eternity

III. Generous giving brings joy to God (vss. 18-19)

From commerce to the temple:

1) *"A fragrant offering"*

- Something very beautiful

- Expression used for Christ's offering of Himself for us (Ephesians 5:2)

- Offering to God as all is His in the first place

2) *"An acceptable sacrifice"*

- We cannot earn salvation—only the sacrifice of Jesus on the cross does that

- Giving is an act of worship which liberates us from the hold money can have

- Giving helps set us free

3) *"Pleasing to God"*

- Kindness to a child pleases the parents—it pleases God when we give to His children

The New Testament encourages us to give:

- Regularly (1 Corinthians 16:2)

- Proportionately

- Joyfully

Context of verse 19 is generous giving

One of the most wonderful promises of the Bible can only be claimed by those who fulfill conditions

- *"My God..."*
Signifies a personal relationship

- *"...will meet..."*
Means literally "fill up by adding"

- *"...all your needs..."*
Not wants, but needs, including material ones—we are freed from worry

- *"...according to his glorious riches..."*
In a manner that befits His wealth

We cannot outgive God

Notes

Notes

Conclusion (vss. 20-23)

Letter begins and ends with grace (Philippians 1:2; 4:23)

Summarizes essence of Christianity

Central theme of this letter, the New Testament, and the Bible as a whole is God's love and generosity

Last four verses of Philippians summarize the teaching of the book:

- Love for God:
  desire to see God's name glorified (vs. 20)

- Love for others:
  Paul sends his greetings to each one of God's people (vs. 21)

- God's love for us:
  Jesus is the channel of all the good gifts that come to us

Paul prays for the *"the grace of the Lord Jesus Christ "* (vs. 23) to be with them

His love enables us to love Him and to love others

He is the source of our love

Why is 'Life Worth Living'?
Answer: JESUS CHRIST

Recommended reading
The Greatest Thing in the World
Henry Drummond
Bridge Logos Publishers
0-8827-0763-9

Other Resources

Alpha™ books by Nicky Gumbel:

Questions of Life

The Alpha course in book form. In 15 compelling chapters the author points the way to an authentic Christianity that is exciting and relevant to today's world.

Searching Issues

The seven issues most often raised by participants of Alpha: suffering, other religions, sex before marriage, the New Age, homosexuality, science and Christianity, and the Trinity.

Challenging Lifestyle

An in-depth look at the Sermon on the Mount (Matthew 5—7). The author shows that Jesus' teaching flies in the face of modern lifestyle and presents us with a radical alternative.

The Heart of Revival

Ten Bible studies on the Book of Isaiah, drawing out important truths for today by interpreting some of the teaching of the Old Testament prophet Isaiah. The book seeks to understand what revival might mean and how we can prepare to be part of it.

30 Days

Nicky Gumbel selects 30 passages from the Old and New Testaments which can be read over 30 days. It is designed for those taking an *Alpha*™ course and others who are interested in beginning to explore the Bible.

For more information on *Alpha*™, including details of tapes, videos, and training manuals, contact David C. Cook Church Ministries, 4050 Lee Vance View, Colorado Springs, CO 80918.

For *Alpha*™ orders, call toll-free 1-800-36-ALPHA.